The Story of Our Past

SOCIAL SCIENCE PUPIL BOOK

Published by Department of Education Papua New Guinea

First Published 1987
Reprinted 1988, 1993, 1994, 1995, 1996 (three times), 1997, 1998, 1999 (three times), 2000 (twice), 2002, 2007, 2008 (twice), 2015 (D)

ISBN 9980 58048 8
ISBN 978 9980 58048 1
National Library of Papua New Guinea

Cover photograph: Dr Wilhelm Wendland, medical officer of the German administration, outside the Hotel First Bismarck, Herbertshöhe (Kokopo) in 1906. (Mitchell Library State Library of New South Wales)

Typeset by Syarikat Seng Teik Sdn. Bhd., Malaysia
Printed in Australia by Ligare Pty Ltd
Published by Department of Education, Papua New Guinea
Prepared by Oxford University Press
253 Normanby Road, South Melbourne, Australia

Acknowledgements

This book was written by Andrew Mickleburgh. The Papua New Guinea Department of Education acknowledges the contribution of many individuals at the Curriculum Unit and on the Social Science Syllabus Advisory Committee to the trialling and review of the book. The participation of the teachers and students at the trial schools—Mongop, Laloki, Tapini, Kimbe, Goroka, Muaina, Kilakila, Badihagwa, and Gerehu Provincial High Schools—is greatly appreciated.

The textbook development work was co-ordinated by the late Greg Chariton, in the earlier stages, and subsequently by Mike McRory, Senior Curriculum Officer for Social Science at the Curriculum Unit.

The publisher wishes to thank the following people and organisations for supplying, and granting permission to reproduce, photographs:

Post Courier, pp. 2, 5 (top), 21 (left), 36 (centre), 37 (top), 38, 42, 50; National Library of Papua New Guinea pp. 5 (top), 19, 21 (right), 27, 28, 29, 32; Word Publishing pp. 5 (bottom), 9, 35, 44, 47, 48; University of Papua New Guinea pp. 6 (bottom left and right), 14; La Trobe Library, State Library of Victoria p. 17; Royal Commonwealth Society p. 20; Australian War Memorial, pp. 22, 32. The extract from R.J. Blong, The Time of Darkness, ANU Press, Canberra, 1982, is reproduced by permission of Pergamon Press Australia.

Secretary's Message

The topic **Growth of Our Country** is the second term's work in the Grade Seven Provincial High School Social Science Course. It is the first of the four topics which develop the theme **Change** through Grades Seven to Ten.

The book is the core learning material for the topic. A supporting set of teaching notes is available. The teaching notes advise the teachers on how to make the best use of the pupil's book.

The material in the book integrates the presentation of information, the development of ideas, reinforcement and application of Social Science skills and the fostering of attitudes.

Three types of activities appear at the end of each section. There are Exercises to ensure comprehension of the material; there are Things to Discuss and Things to Do. The activities combine work on sections of the book with direct investigations both inside and outside school.

This book is one of the items of instructional material produced for Provincial High Schools in Papua New Guinea as part of the Education III Textbook Sub-Project.

S G ROAKEINA
Secretary for Education

Contents

1. What is History?

History is the study of the past.

People who study the past are known as **historians**. They ask questions such as: "Where did the people of Papua New Guinea come from?" and "Why do we live the way we do today?"

Why Do We Study History?

We study history so that we can know some of the things that made our country what it is today. When we know our history well, we will be able to make better plans for the future.

Learning history helps us understand our **customs** and **traditions**. It helps us to be proud of our country and the people in it. Learning history is also a little like learning from our mistakes. We see where something went wrong before and we try not to make the same mistakes again.

Why Study History?	
Arguments For the Study of History	**Arguments Against the Study of History**
For example: • It will help us to understand and be proud of our customs and traditions. • It will help us learn from our mistakes.	For example: • It does not help us to get a job. • It looks at things that happened in the past. We should think of the future.

The way people live is changing all the time. The way people live today in Papua New Guinea is changing very quickly. This has caused some problems. Some people think that the old ways are no longer important. Many people are worried about their future because of all the changes that are taking place.

The history of Papua New Guinea will help all of us to understand why these people have worries. It can help us to make good changes that will help Papua New Guinea and its people. This is why we study the story of our past.

How Do Historians Study the Past?

Historians study the past in many ways. Sometimes they can use **written records** such as newspapers, reports, letters, and cave paintings. Stories, songs, and poetry can provide useful information known as **oral** or **spoken history**.

Historians also learn from the things people leave behind them. This means that the places where people lived in the past can also give useful information. In these places historians sometimes find old tools, weapons, and household rubbish. These things are called **artifacts**. Artifacts also give us an idea of how people lived in the past. Often artifacts are very old and in poor condition. But historians are a little like policemen looking for clues. They can use small pieces of information about the past to build up a picture of what things were like then.

Information from other scientists is also used by historians.

Digging for artifacts, Morobe Province.

Warning!

If you ever find any artifacts that may be of interest to historians, please write to the National Museum. We need these artifacts to give us information about the way we lived in the past.

It is against the law for people to touch places such as old village sites and burial grounds.

Why is it important to look after those things that could help us in our study of history?

These cave paintings are an important written record.

An Example of Oral History

Here is a story told by Serave, a Kamano-Kafe man from Eastern Highlands Province.

"I am going to tell the story of darkness. I am going to tell the story of the great darkness which appeared on this ground. I did not see it. People told me and so I know it.

It was while they were asleep, in the night, that it was so dark on this earth, and they slept for about three nights. And when they took flares and went up the hills and made signs, going with flares in the pitch blackness, they said: Can you see my flare? But the flares did not light up the place! So they said: No!

They went on doing that and one time as they were going with a flare there was a little light. And they saw it and said: Ah, now it's getting light! We can see shadows! And they rejoiced greatly. It was a bit light and they were rejoicing and they could see the flares and while they went on rejoicing it became light.

It became light and in the morning and they looked and a lot of stuff like ash had completely "disappeared" the gardens! It had completely covered everything and pigs, animals, rats, every living creature in the scrub and in the woods came out in the open—cassowaries and so forth, too, and they died, and in the morning the people saw them. And they smelt the stench of the creatures which were rotting. And they took the creatures which were still alive and ate them. And they called the stuff which covered everything tanoza [rubbish]. They thought: it is tano ash.

(Tano is a harvest celebration in which an enormous fire is built, producing a lot of ash. The fall of ash reminded the Kamano-Kafe people of this.)

A Huli **legend** from Tari in Southern Highlands Province tells how crops grew better after a fall of volcanic ash. The crops grew so much better that the Dindi gamu ceremony is still performed in the hope that ash will fall to make the soils fertile once more.

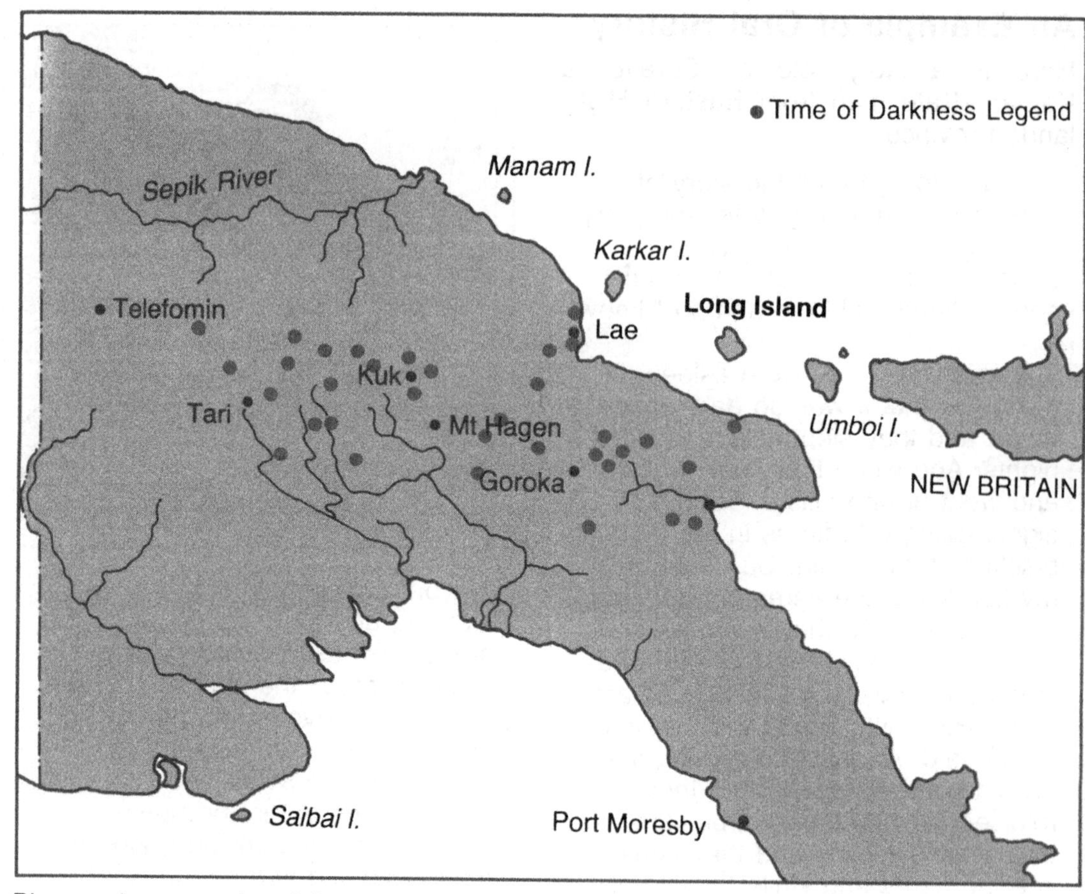

Places where people tell Time of Darkness legends.

What can we learn from these stories? The legends tell us that there was a huge volcanic **eruption** at some time in the past. This was so big that, even in a country with many volcanoes, the story of this eruption is still told today.

Geologists are scientists who study the rocks and the earth. They tell historians that in the ground in many parts of Papua New Guinea there is a thin layer of volcanic ash. This is found throughout about 100,000 km^2 of our country. They believe this ash is from the eruption of Long Island 300 years ago. This idea is supported by legends from many other parts of Papua New Guinea. All the places where people tell of this eruption are to the west of Long Island. This means that the legends tell us not only how the volcano affected the lives of the people, but also which direction the winds were blowing at the time. This is one example of how historians can use oral history to find out what has happened in our past.

Another example is from one Motu village near Port Moresby. The people tell a story of the destruction of a village and the building of a new village in another place. Other people did not believe this at first, but historians have now found Motu artifacts where the legend said the village was. The age of the village can be dated by tracing back the chief's family. Scientists have since shown that this is the true age of the village.

Activities

Exercises

1. Eight important words about history are hidden in the puzzle below. Make a list of the words which you are able to find.

A R E N A P E O P L E
L O S H U M O N A D E
A R T I F A C T S M C
N A E S R P R I T R U
O L E T I U I M A L S
O O M O S A G O Y A T
R A O R T N A H A N O
B E V I D E N C E E M
A S T A A W T E N S S
C H A N G E N M A I A

2. In your own words, list two reasons why it is important to study the history of Papua New Guinea.
3. List three ways that historians collect information about the past.

Things to Discuss

1. As a class, talk about some of the ways that you could get information about the history of your area.
2. Imagine that a person dug up your school rubbish dump 50 years from now. What sort of things do you think the person could say about your school from this **evidence**?
3. What lessons could we learn from this historical event that could help people today?

This is Mount Lamington in Oro Province. It erupted in 1951, killing 3,500 people. People continued to live near Mount Lamington, even though they knew it could erupt.

Many people were killed as they fled the eruption.

Things to Do

1. Ask an old person about a story from your area.
   - **(a)** Write down this story.
   - **(b)** What does this story tell you about your people?
   - **(c)** Display the stories that you have collected on your classroom notice board.
2. Look at each of these photographs. What information could each of these photographs tell us about the way these people live?

2. The Island of New Guinea

Where Did Our Land Come From?

The island of New Guinea is the second largest island in the world. Papua New Guinea is the eastern half of this island, plus many smaller islands. Irian Jaya, which is part of Indonesia, is the western half of this island.

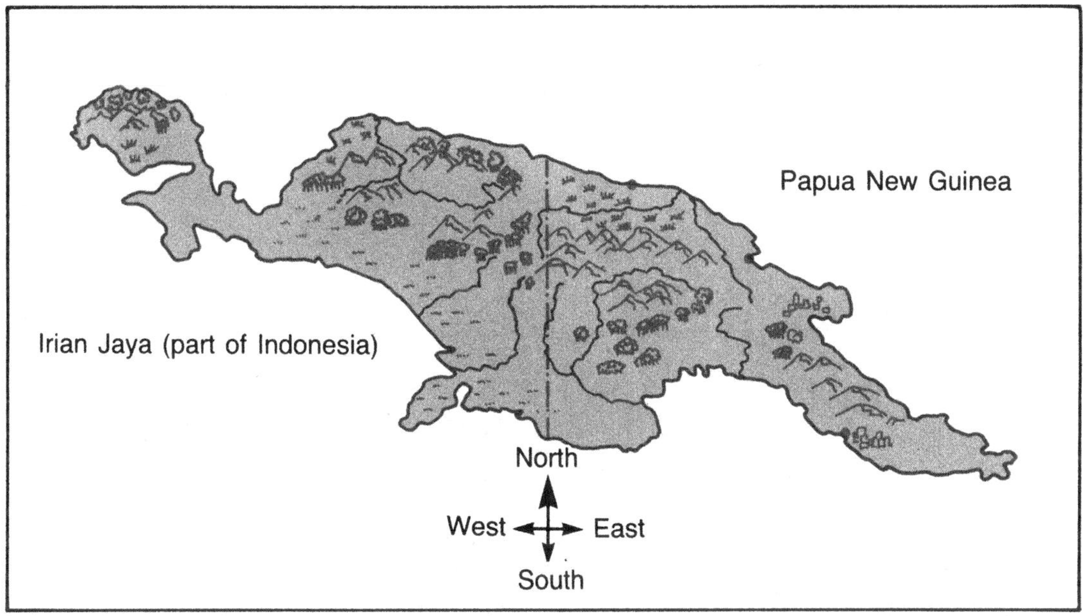

The island of New Guinea.

How old is Papua New Guinea?

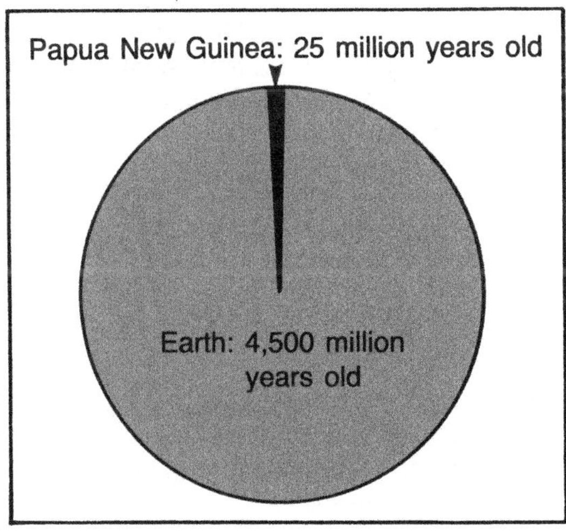

Geologists are people who study the earth and how it was made. Geologists think that the earth is about 4,500 million years old. They think the island of New Guinea is about 25 million years old.

Twenty-five million years ago the island of New Guinea was just a small number of volcanoes. These volcanoes were slowly pushed up out of the sea. The volcanoes continued to erupt for about 12 million years. More and more land came out of the sea. About 13 million years ago Papua New Guinea began to get the shape that it has today.

25 million years ago.

13 million years ago.

Changing Sea Levels

The earth's climate has changed over time. It has sometimes been much colder than it is today. About 3 million years ago it became so cold that a lot of water in the sea was frozen into ice. Because a lot of ice formed on the land as well, the amount of water left in the sea became less and the sea level fell. Land which had been covered by the sea was now dry. During these cold periods New Guinea and Australia were joined as one land. Geologists call this land **Sahul**.

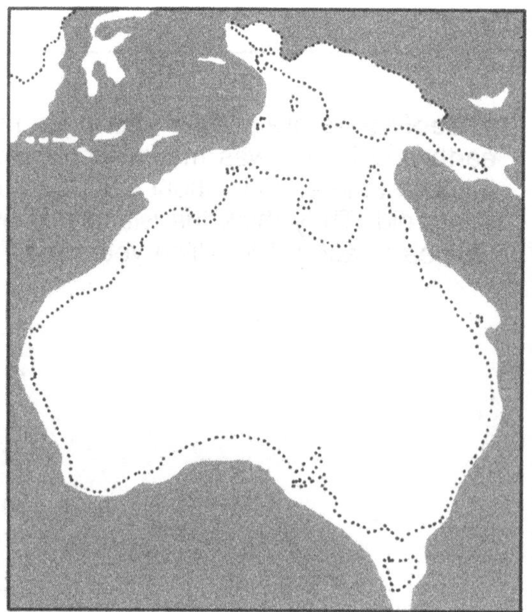
The land of Sahul.

In this map the land of Sahul is shown in white. The coastlines of New Guinea and Australia as we know them today are shown by dotted lines.

Activities

Exercises

1. Look at the diagram at the bottom of page 7. In your own words, describe the age of Papua New Guinea compared to the rest of the earth.
2. The words to complete this paragraph are hidden in the puzzle below. See how many of these words you can find.

The earth is very ________ . The islands of what is now Papua New Guinea were made when ________ erupted. The ________ of our country has changed over time. Once Papua New Guinea and ______ were joined by land. This happened during a time when ________ were much lower. The large land that was made because of this is called ________.

A	P	A	P	V	O	L	A	N	A	M
O	O	T	E	O	P	A	N	A	U	A
R	S	E	A	L	E	V	E	L	S	O
L	T	R	A	C	E	O	R	A	T	N
E	A	S	H	A	P	E	S	I	R	S
G	N	A	E	N	E	E	D	O	A	T
E	E	H	C	O	L	D	E	R	L	R
A	R	U	L	E	N	I	P	O	I	I
S	O	L	D	S	T	A	N	D	A	T

Things to Discuss

1. You are a historian. You are looking for things that could show that Papua New Guinea and Australia were once joined together. What sort of things would you look for that might be almost the same in both countries?
2. As a class, discuss how this photograph looks. How has our land changed since then?

A volcanic landscape. The whole of Papua New Guinea may once have looked like this.

Things to Do

1. **(a)** Find a small glass jar. Stand a small piece of wood or a stone with a flat top in the jar. Slowly fill the jar about half full with water. On the outside of the jar mark the level of the water.

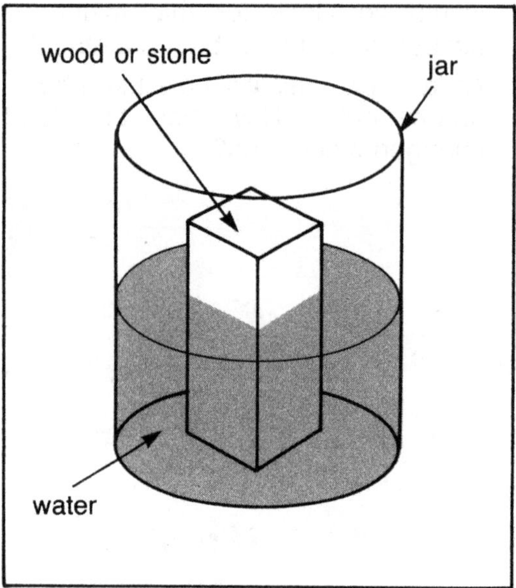

   (b) Remove some of the water from the jar and place this water in a freezer. Mark the new level of the water on the outside of the jar. Notice how some of the wood that was under water is now above the water.

   (c) Once the water that was taken out of the jar is frozen, remove it from the freezer. Place the ice on top of the piece of wood. As the ice melts, see how the level of water in the jar rises and covers part of the wood that was dry before.

   (d) As a class, talk about how this experiment helps us to understand why Papua New Guinea and Australia were once joined.

2. Trace the map of Sahul on p. 8. Colour in New Guinea and Australia. Use the same colour for both. Use a different colour to show those parts of Sahul that were once dry but are now under water.

3. The First People

To find out when the first people came to Papua New Guinea, historians use information found by **archaeologists**. Archaeologists are scientists who study places where people lived long ago. With the help of many other scientists they now think people may have been living in Papua New Guinea for over 50,000 years. As archaeologists collect new evidence they may find that people have been living in Papua New Guinea for even longer than this.

Land area 50,000 years ago

---- Possible route taken by the first people who came to Papua New Guinea and Australia

Where Did the First Papua New Guineans Come From?

Historians think that the first people came to Papua New Guinea from South-East Asia. Even though New Guinea and Australia were joined by land at that time, some of the islands to the west of New Guinea were still separated by water. To get to New Guinea the people used rafts and canoes to cross the water between these islands. The people came in small groups over thousands of years. Later some of these people crossed the land bridge from New Guinea and settled in Australia.

This map shows the way that the first people came to New Guinea and Australia.

Possible route taken by the first people to come to Papua New Guinea.

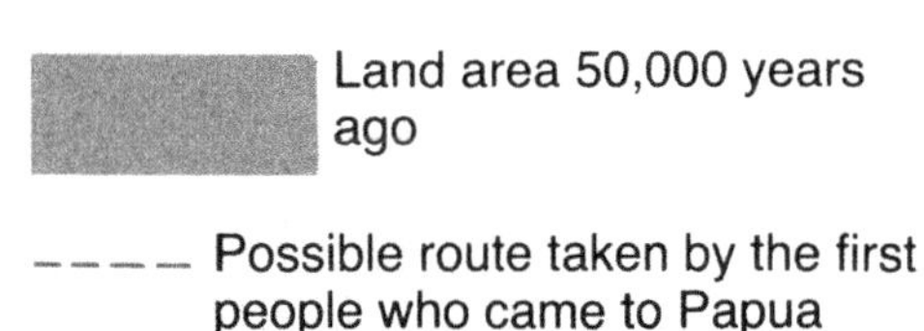

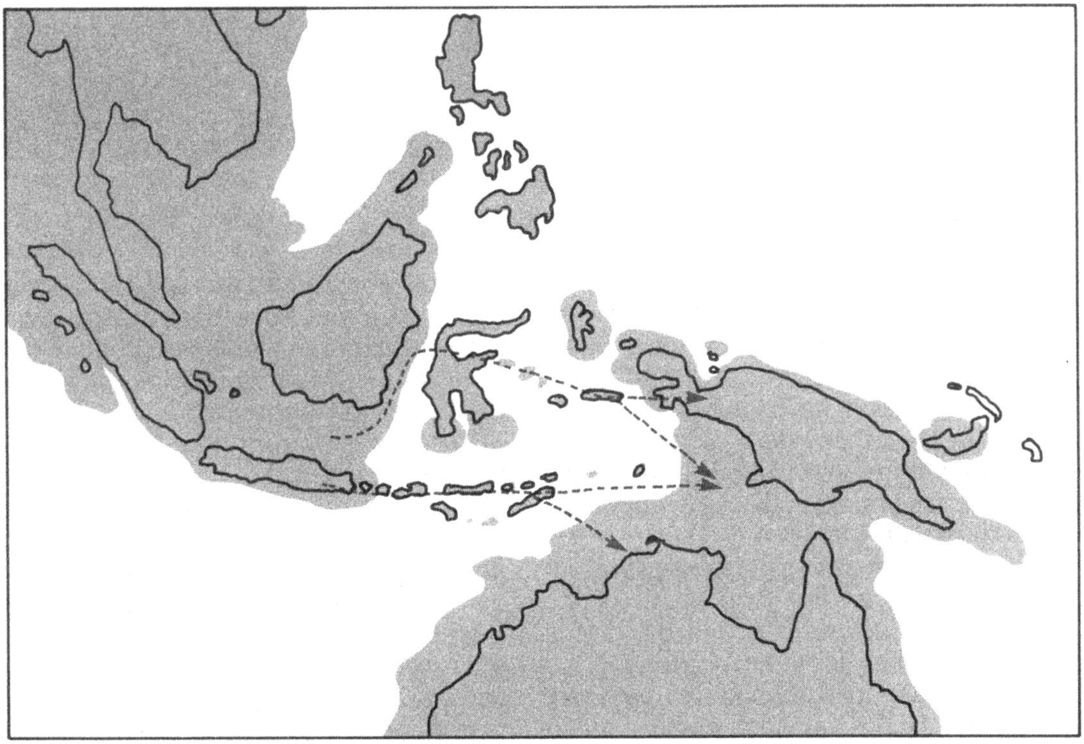

These first people may have brought with them some Asian plants such as taro. When they came to Papua New Guinea they found coconuts and bananas which they had known and used in their old home. But they also learnt to eat foods, like pitpit and sago, which were new to them.

This map shows where some of our important foods came from.

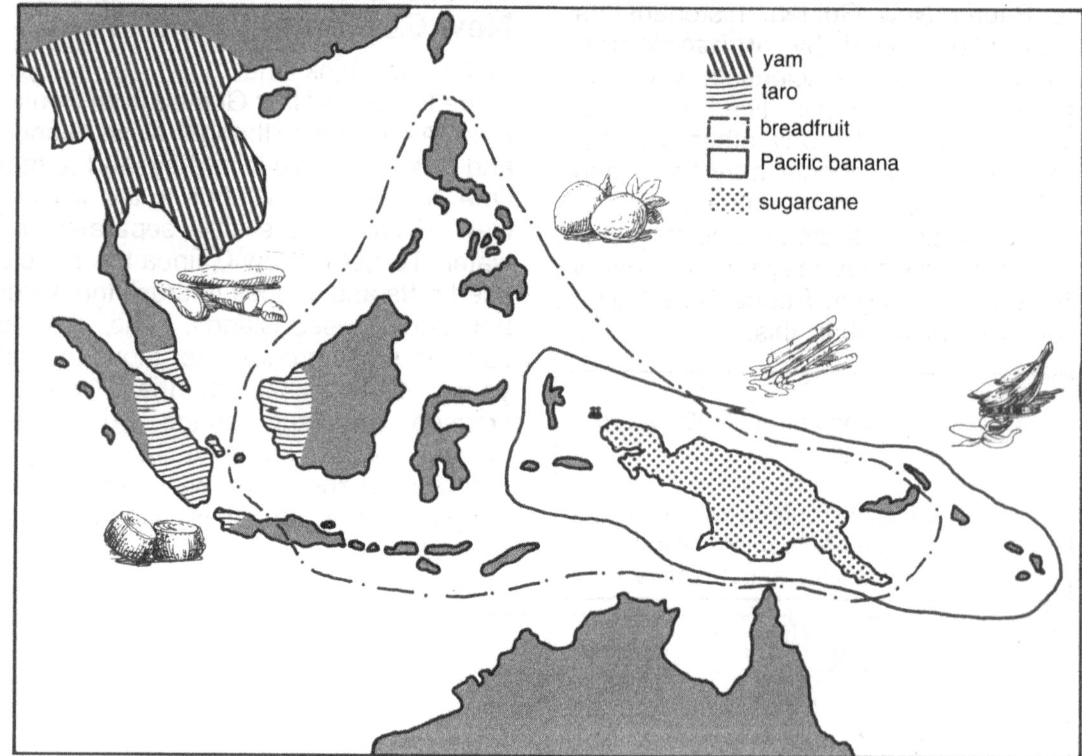

Where some of our important foods came from.

How Did These People Live?

There is evidence to show that there were not many animals to hunt when the first people arrived in Papua New Guinea. These people had to collect a lot of their food from plants, although there were not as many different food plants as there are today. Fishing in the sea and rivers was also an important way of getting food.

Over thousands of years people learnt to plant and care for food plants. They learnt to cut down trees and dig drains to bring water to their gardens. This made it easier for the people to get food.

Most of the places where these people might have made their gardens are now covered by the sea. So a lot of evidence about how these people lived is lost. But not in all places. In the Huon Peninsula in Morobe Province, the land has been pushed up out of the sea. There, people from the University of Papua New Guinea have found stone axes that are 37,000 years old. They think people used these axes to cut down forest trees so that gardens could be made. They are looking for even more evidence because the age of these axes suggests that the first people of Papua New Guinea were amongst the first people in the whole world to be gardeners.

Activities

Exercises

1. Which of the foods in the photograph opposite:
   (a) have always been grown in Papua New Guinea?
   (b) were brought to Papua New Guinea from somewhere else?

The map on page 12 will help you answer this question. Write your answer in a table like this:

Foods which have always been in Papua New Guinea	**Foods which were brought to Papua New Guinea from Somewhere Else**

2. Use the letters provided in the clue to complete each of the following statements:
   (a) The first Papua New Guineans probably came from ________.
   clue: S A A I
   (b) The first Papua New Guineans were hunters, gatherers, and ________.
   clue: N I S H F E M R E
   (c) Papua New Guineans may have been some of the first people in the world to make ________.
   clue: S A D R E G N
   (d) ________ are a food which has always been found in Papua New Guinea.
   clue: N A B A A N S
   (e) Papua New Guinea was once part of a very old land called ________.
   clue: L A H S U
   (f) Scientists who study places where people lived in the past are called ________.
   clue:
   E O G I A H C R A L O T S S

Things to Discuss

1. As a class, see if you can think of any reasons why people from South-East Asia came to Sahul over 50,000 years ago.

Things to Do

1. Use arrows and labels to show the correct position on the time-line of each of the following events. For example, kaukau was first brought to Papua New Guinea about 300 years ago. This is shown with an arrow and label pointing at 300 years.

   over 50,000 years ago: First people came to Papua New Guinea.
   37,000 years ago: Stone axe heads made by people on the Huon Peninsula; probably used to clear forests for gardening.
   26,000 years ago: People at Kosipe in Central Province used stone axes to clear forests for gardening.
   20,000 years ago: Land between New Guinea and Australia covered by sea.
   9,000 years ago: Gardeners in the Wahgi Valley, Western Highlands Province.
   6,000 years ago: Pigs brought to Papua New Guinea.

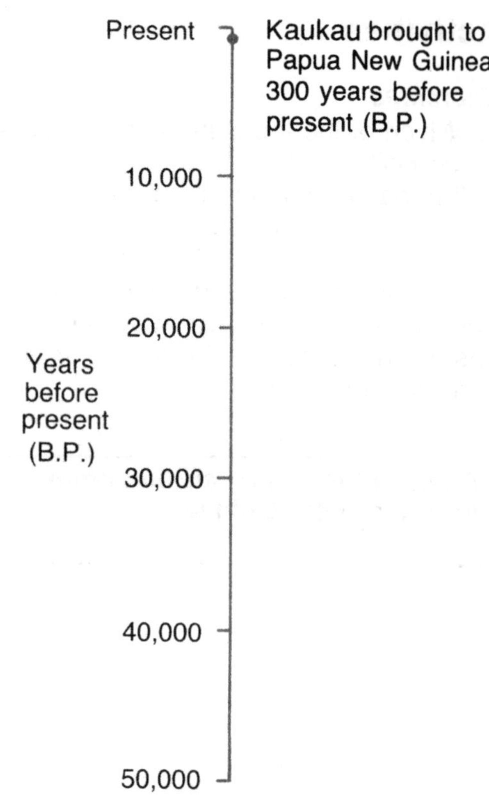

2. Look at this photograph of a man in the Wahgi Valley. Draw a picture to show:
   (a) where the man is standing;
   (b) the present level of the land;
   (c) the old drain. (The old drain is marked with white pegs.)

   After you have drawn your picture write two or three sentences to explain how you think the gardeners who made these drains a long time ago lived.

4. The Arrival of Foreigners

The First Outsiders

Our **ancestors** have lived in Papua New Guinea for at least 50,000 years. Historians are not sure when our ancestors were first visited by people from other countries. The earliest visit that historians know about was by people from Asia 1,200 years ago. For the next 1,000 years, Chinese, Malays, and people from what is now Indonesia visited both the north and south coast of New Guinea. Even today, oral history in parts of East and West Sepik Provinces says that the first "outsiders" who came to these areas were Malay **traders.**

Our first visitors were traders from nearby Asian countries.

European Explorers

The first Europeans to sail past the island of New Guinea were Portuguese and Spanish **explorers**. In 1526 Jorge de Meneses, a Portuguese, visited the western coast of Irian Jaya. He called the country Ilhos dos Papuas, or Islands of the Papuans. The word "Papuan" comes from a Malay word which means frizzy or curly haired.

In the early 1600s most of the European explorers were Dutchmen from Holland. Most were looking for **spices** which were used for flavour in European cooking. They did not find many spices in New Guinea and did not stay very long. Later, however, the Dutch took control of the part of New Guinea which we now call Irian Jaya.

In the 1700s English and French ships came to Papua New Guinea. In 1700 an Englishman named Dampier became the first European to see New Britain. He was followed in 1767 by another Englishman named Carteret. In 1768 a Frenchman named Bougainville explored parts of the coast of New Britain, New Ireland, Manus, Buka, and Bougainville.

This map shows where some of the European explorers in the Pacific sailed between 1500 and 1800.

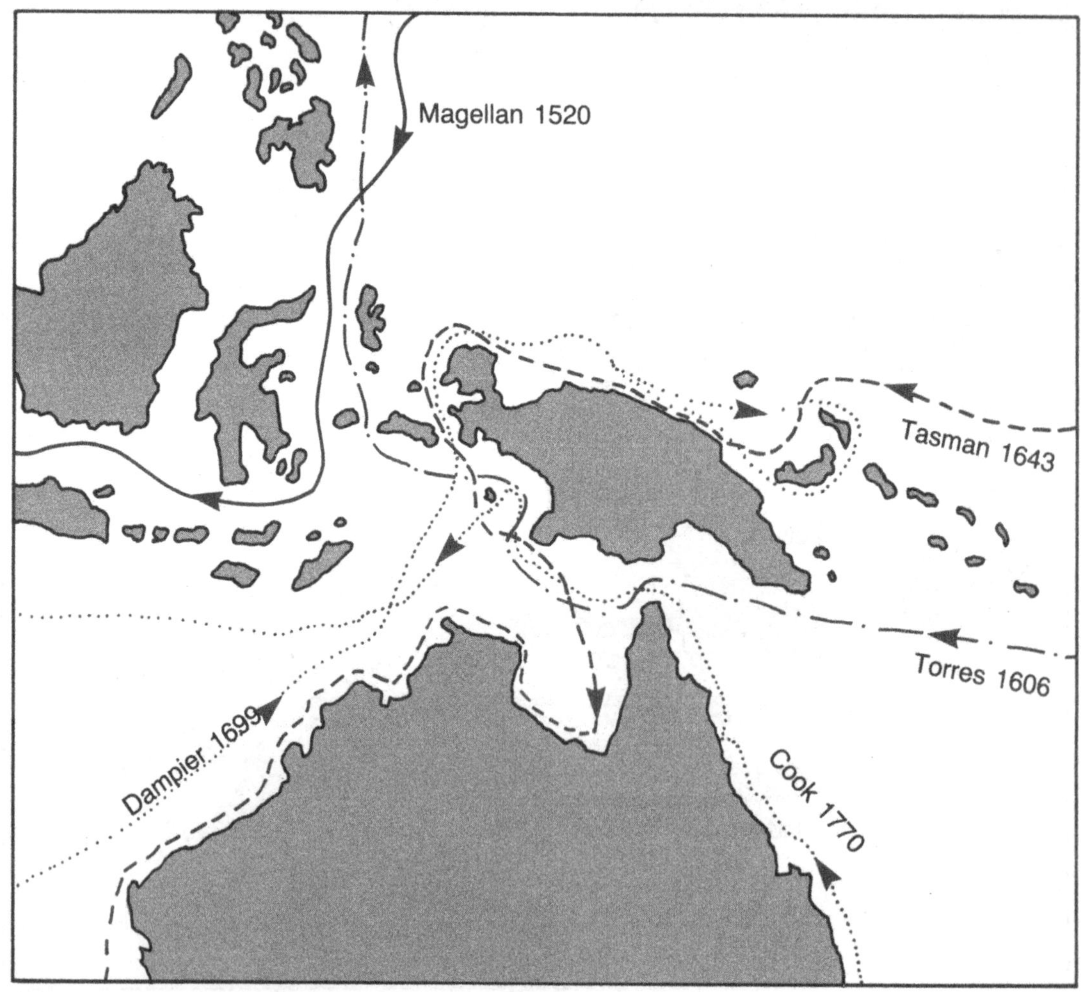

Where some of the European explorers sailed.

Other Reasons Why Foreigners Came to Papua New Guinea

Not all the new visitors were explorers. Some people came to **trade**, to get goods such as sandalwood and mother-of-pearl shell. In return they gave Papua New Guineans such things as cloth, metal axes, and knives.

One group which came to Papua New Guinea was the **labour recruiters**. These men were looking for people to work on plantations in Queensland (Australia), Fiji, and Samoa. In the 1870s and 1880s about 5,000 Papua New Guineans were taken to work on plantations in other countries.

Another group of people who came to Papua New Guinea were the **missionaries**. In 1606 fourteen children from Mailu were taken to the Philippines by the Spanish explorer Torres. There they were given a Christian baptism. But it was not until the 1800s that the work of the missionaries really began in Papua New Guinea.

Labour recruiting in the Island provinces.

The map below shows the date when some of the first missions in Papua New Guinea were started.

Most of the early contact between white people and Papua New Guineans was in the coastal areas. People who lived away from the coast did not see white people until many years later.

In the next chapter we shall see how a European system of **government** was started in Papua New Guinea.

Location of the first missions.

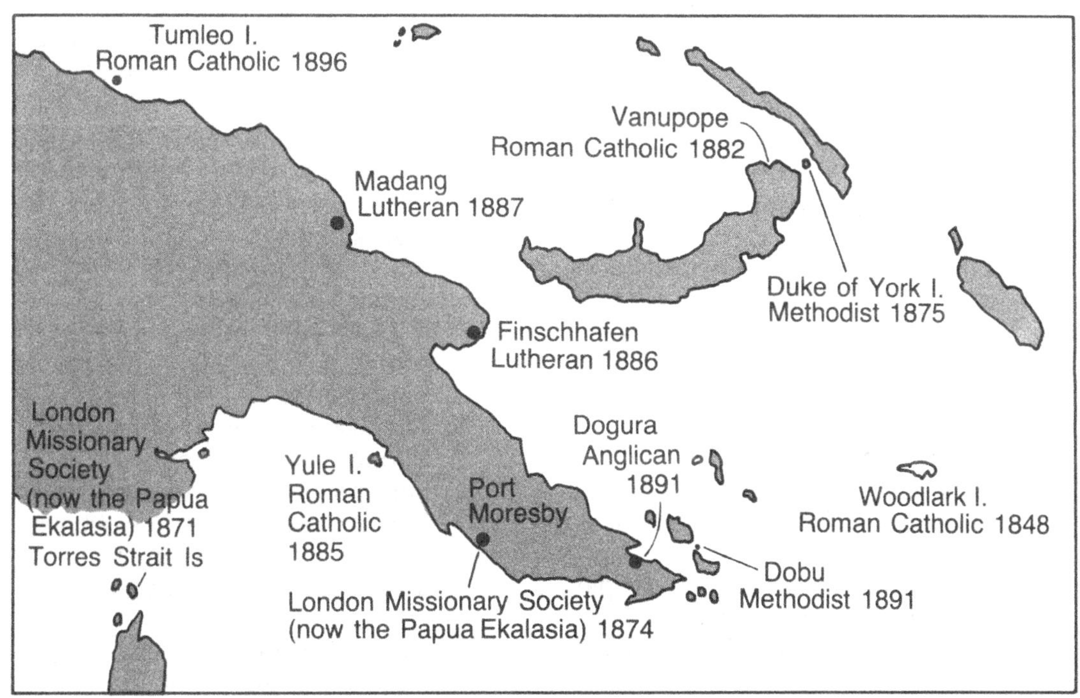

Activities

Exercises

1. Copy and complete the crossword puzzle below.

Across

1. The first ________ who were not ancestors of today's Papua New Guineans probably visited Papua New Guinea about 1,200 years ago.
5. Most early contact between white people and Papua New Guineans was along the ______.
6. Some of the white people who came to visit Papua New Guinea were ________.
9. Some of the first white people to come to Papua New Guinea were ________ recruiters.
10. Area from which the first "outsiders" came to Papua New Guinea.
13. Same clue as 6 Across.
15. Nationality of some of the early European explorers—spelt backwards!
16. The arrival of the white people started a period of great ______ in the lives of Papua New Guineans.
17. Large ocean to the east of Papua New Guinea.

Down

1. Malay word meaning frizzy or curly haired.
2. Nationality of the first white person to see the island of New Guinea.
3. Some Papua New Guineans were taken to this country in the 1870s and 1880s to work on plantations.
4. Early Europeans travelled to Papua New Guinea by ______.
7. A European country from which some of the early explorers of Papua New Guinea came.
8. The first mission to be started in Papua New Guinea.
11. First part of the name of one of Papua New Guinea's neighbours.
12. The people in 8 Down wanted to tell Papua New Guineans about ________ .
14. Type of transport used by the early European explorers.

2. One group of people who came to Papua New Guinea were explorers. Why did these explorers come to Papua New Guinea?

Name three other types of people who came to Papua New Guinea and explain why each of them came.

Write your answer in a table like this:

People who Came to Papua New Guinea	Reason for Coming
1. Explorers 2. 3. 4.	

Things to Discuss

1. You are living near the coast in Papua New Guinea a long time ago. You have just seen, for the first time, a group of white people come from a large boat and land near your village.

   As a class, talk about the feelings that:

   (a) you might have had when you first saw these people;

   (b) the white people might have had when they landed in Papua New Guinea.

Things to Do

1. Write a short story of between 50 and 80 words about the people in this old drawing. The story should say something about:

   (a) the reasons why white people came to Papua New Guinea;

   (b) some of the feelings that Papua New Guineans and white people might have had when they first saw each other.

2. Complete the table below.

The early explorers

Date	Name of Explorer	Nationality
1526	de Meneses	
	Torres	
1700		English
1767		English
	Bougainville	

5. Britain, Germany, Australia, and Papua New Guinea

There have been many types of traditional government in Papua New Guinea for thousands of years. Traditional leaders such as bigmen and chiefs helped their people in the same way as leaders in the government today. The type of government which we have in Papua New Guinea now was started by Europeans and Australians.

Papua

In 1883 Queensland in Australia tried to take control of Papua. Queensland was frightened that the many Germans in New Guinea would get the German government to take control of Papua and New Guinea. At that time Queensland was a **colony** of Britain and so did not have the power to take control of Papua. Instead, Australia asked Britain to make Papua a British **Protectorate**. This meant that Britain agreed to help Papua without making Papua a part of Britain. Papua became a British Protectorate in 1884.

In 1906 Britain gave the newly **independent** country of Australia the work of governing Papua, which Australia did until 1975.

This photograph was taken when Papua became a British Protectorate on 6 November 1884.

Sir Peter Scratchley—the man in charge of the Protectorate.

Sir William MacGregor—the first governor of Papua.

New Guinea

New Guinea was a colony of Germany for thirty years. From 1885 to 1899 the colony was controlled by a business called the **New Guinea Company**. The owners of this business lived in Germany. They had many plantations and trading stations in New Guinea.

In 1899 the German government took the power to control New Guinea away from the New Guinea Company. The German government continued to govern New Guinea until 1914.

During the First World War, Germany lost control of New Guinea. From 1914 until 1921 New Guinea was governed by Australian soldiers. In 1921 the **League of Nations** asked Australia to continue to govern New Guinea. The League of Nations is now called the United Nations.

Albert Hahl, the administrator of German New Guinea, photographed with his wife.

The Territories of Papua and New Guinea

The Territories of Papua and New Guinea were governed separately by Australia until after the Second World War. It was not until the fighting ended that Papua and New Guinea were governed as one country, with its capital at Port Moresby.

Australian soldiers and New Guinea police at Rabaul in 1921.

Activities

Exercises

1. Complete the time-line below. Next to each date marked with a dot name the important event that took place. Write suitable labels to explain how Papua New Guinea was governed between 1921 and 1939, and from 1945 to 1975.

Papua New Guinea: 1880 to the present

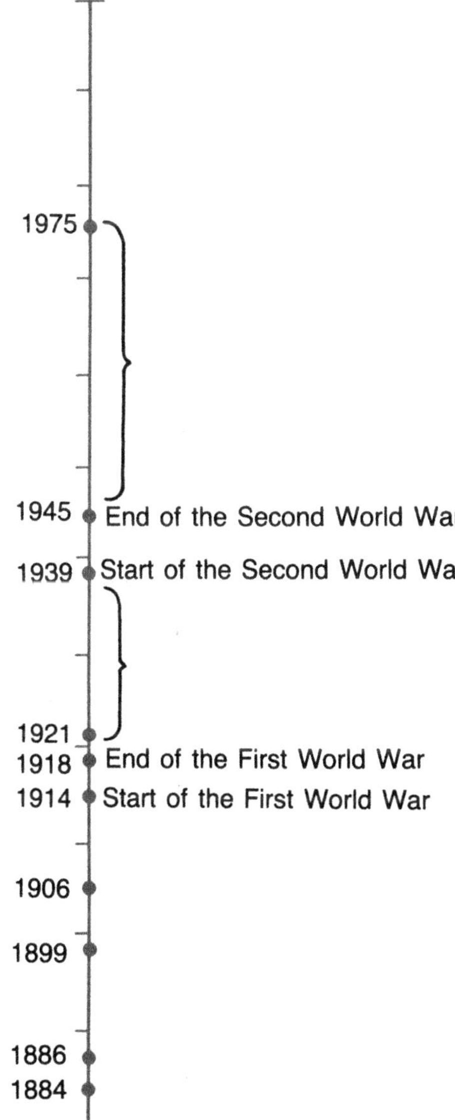

2. Traditional types of government have existed in Papua New Guinea for thousands of years. List three other types of government that have been used in Papua New Guinea since 1880. (These are all described in this chapter.)

Things to Discuss

1. Part of the speech that was made at the time Papua was made a British Protectorate has been simplified below.

> The Queen of England wants me to explain the things you have just seen. These things mean that you will now be cared for by the British Government. Bad people will not be allowed to take away your land or to take you away from your home.
>
> If you have any problems you should tell the Government's men. These men will live with you, listen to your problems and help you. I hope that you understand that we are here as your friends. Always remember that the Queen looks after you and will send good people to look after this Protectorate.
>
> Commodore James Erskine

   (a) What does the word **Protectorate** mean?
   (b) What changes took place when Papua became a Protectorate?
   (c) As a class, discuss whether you think it was good or bad to have made Papua a British Protectorate.

2. Discuss some of the changes that took place when white people came to Papua New Guinea.

Things to Do

1. Until the end of the Second World War, Papua and New Guinea were governed as separate countries.

   The man at the top of this picture is trying to stop people from crossing the border that white people made between Papua and New Guinea.

   Write a story about the way European government came to Papua New Guinea. In this story, say whether or not you think it was a good idea to draw a border between Papua and New Guinea. Give a reason for your answer.

2. Look at the map of German New Guinea below.

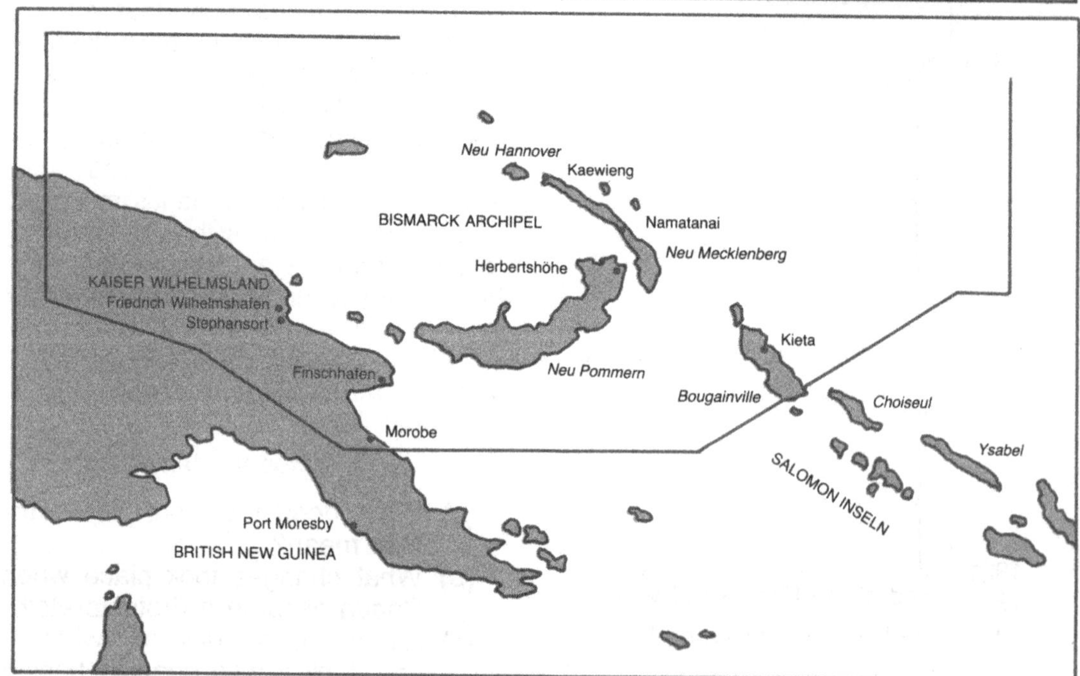

   (a) What did the Germans call mainland New Guinea? Do you know why?
   (b) What did the Germans call New Britain?
   (c) What are the following towns called today:
       - Herbertshohe
       - Friedrich Wilhelmshafen
   (d) Name one town in Papua New Guinea that still has the name given to it by the Germans.

6. A Time of Change

The diagram below shows some of the ways in which the British, German, and later Australian governments tried to gain control over the Papua New Guinean people.

labour recruiters
loss of important groups
e.g. young men

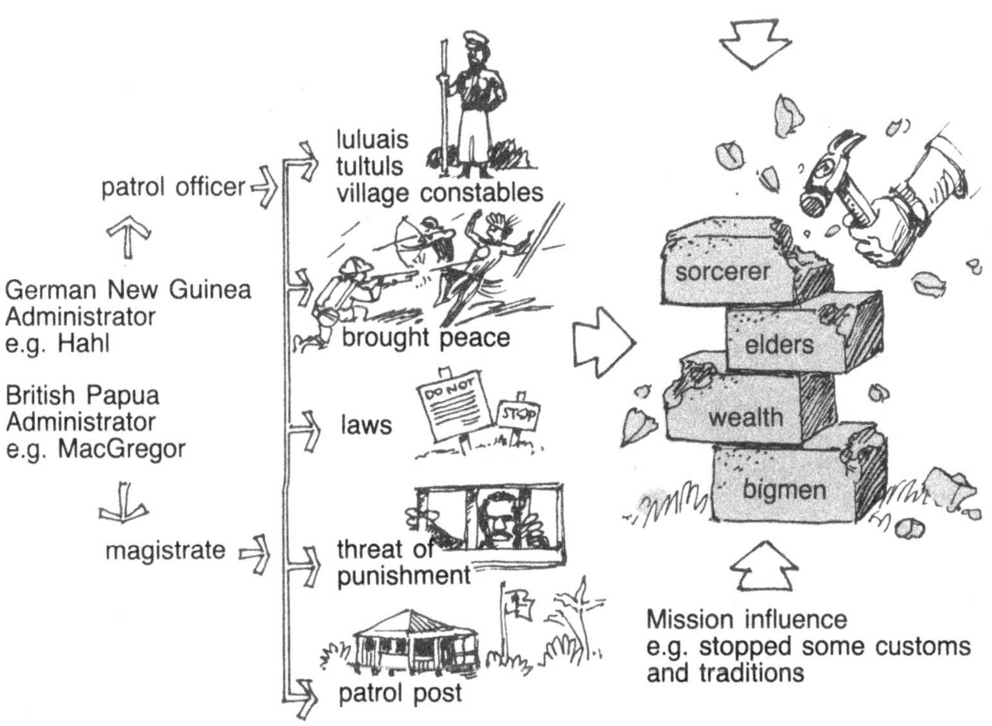

The breakdown of the traditional power structure

Administrators

The person in charge of government and law during the time of European control was called the **Administrator**. In the early days of their rule administrators had a lot of power and made most of the laws themselves.

Sir Hubert Murray:
Acting Administrator of Papua 1907–1909
Lieutenant Governor and Administrator
1909–1940

Patrol Officers

In the past there was a lot of fighting between different tribes and clans. It was necessary to bring peace to these people before the new type of government could work. This was done by government patrols led by a white patrol officer and Papua New Guinean police.

The patrol officers' job was not an easy one. Once peace had been brought to an area, the patrol officer had to build houses, airstrips, and wharves, look after the prison and hospital, and listen to court cases.

The rate of payment for native carriers will be either 6d. per day in cash or 2 sticks of tobacco per day or trade to the value of 6d. per day. In most cases it will be found that in travelling from village to village, the only possible means of payment will be by sticks of tobacco.

Patrol equipment as indicated . . . will be issued to out-stations;

Item	Qty
Tent and Fly, 10 × 12	1
Fly for Carriers, 14 × 16	2
Fly for Police, 14 × 16	2
Hammock (sealed pattern)	1
Swag Bag for Clothes (sealed pattern)	2
Swag Bag for Hammock (sealed pattern)	1
Ground Sheet	1
Food Boxes (trade)	2
Hurricane Lamps	3
Frying-pan	1
Saucepan	1
Billycans	2
Buckets	2
Stools (folding camp)	2
Table (folding)	1
Despatch Box (iron)	1
Medicine Chest	1
Flag, Australian	1
Haversack	1
Waterbottle	1
Revolver	1
Compass, prismatic	1
Protractor	1

All ammunition is to be kept under direct control of a European officer, and is not to be issued to native police by any person except a European officer, who must make such issue personally. . . . All native police on stations and their quarters are to be searched periodically in order to ascertain if they have ammunition in their possession without authority.

Immediately a police patrol enters a native village the Australian Flag will be hoisted outside the quarters of the senior European officer of the patrol. It will be lowered on his departure. During the stay of the patrol it will be hoisted at sunrise and lowered at sunset. . . .

Officers will arrange for an armed guard of any non-commissioned officer (or senior constable) and three constables, together with a constable with side-arms only, to parade at the station or post flagpole at sunrise and sunset. The constable with side-arms will hoist or lower the flag and the guard will present arms as the flag is hoisted or lowered as the case may be.

The Territory of New Guinea District Standing Instructions, 1925

Laws

Many laws made by the administrators went against the people's customs and traditions. However, these laws tried to do many things. Some laws tried to stop people from doing things that hurt other people. For example, laws were made to stop tribal fighting and payback killing. Other laws were made to get the people to do things that the Administrator thought would help them. For example, people were told to bury their dead under the ground to prevent disease, instead of following some of their traditional burial customs. Some laws were made to help the white people; others protected Papua New Guineans.

Luluais, Tultuls, and Village Constables

The administrators chose people to act for the new government and to help patrol officers in the villages.

In New Guinea, the first German governor, Albert Hahl, started the system of **luluais** and **tultuls**. Luluais were often village elders who made sure that the new laws were followed. Tultuls were usually younger men who helped as interpreters.

In Papua, Sir William MacGregor chose **village constables** who did the same work as luluais. MacGregor also chose **village councillors** to look after the interests of the village people.

Luluais, tultuls, village constables and village councillors sometimes went against other village people, such as sorcerers, who were traditionally powerful. They helped to bring the European type of government to many parts of Papua New Guinea. They also helped to break down many of the customs and traditions of the people.

Police in German New Guinea.

A luluai in the Nondugl area in the Western Highlands in 1950.

Those people who broke laws were punished. People sometimes broke the new laws if they thought they could do this without being discovered. The new laws brought many changes to the lives of Papua New Guineans.

Labour Recruiters

In Chapter 4 we saw how people were taken from many parts of Papua New Guinea to work on plantations in other countries. Other people left their villages to work for the government as policemen. Many people were taken to work on plantations or with gold miners in other parts of the country.

Most of the people who left their villages were young men. When they left their villages these young men lost the chance to learn the customs and traditions of their people. When these young men came back to their villages they often brought many new goods and ideas.

Missions

The missions tried to stop people from following some of their old customs and traditions. The missions chose men called **catechists** or **evangelists** to help them. Catechists sometimes went against the traditional village leaders.

A mission teacher from Samoa. He is working on Karkar Island, Madang province.

A catechist.

Most of the schools in Papua New Guinea before the Second World War were started by missions. The missions also helped to start businesses in many parts of Papua New Guinea.

All the things discussed in this chapter caused big changes in the lives of Papua New Guineans. In the next chapter we shall look at an event that caused the biggest change of all: the Second World War.

Activities

Exercises

1. Explain three ways in which the British, German, and Australian governments tried to gain control over the Papua New Guinean people. (The diagram on page 25 shows some of these.)
2. List five changes that took place in the lives of Papua New Guineans under the European and Australian administrations.

Things to Discuss

1. Imagine that you were a patrol officer.
   (a) What feelings might you have had as you went into an area where the people had never seen a white person?
   (b) What would you do when you arrived in this new area?
   (c) How do you think the village people would behave when they first saw you? Why?
2. Discuss the **opinion** that the new type of government could never have been started in Papua New Guinea without the help of Papua New Guineans.

Patrol officers.

Things to Do

1. List three good things and three bad things that happened as a result of having the new type of government in Papua New Guinea.

   Write your answer in a table like this:

European-style Government in Papua New Guinea	
Good Things that Happened as a Result of the New Type of Government	**Bad Things that Happened as a Result of the New Type of Government**

2. Ask your teacher if you can see the films **First Contact** or **Pearls and Savages**.

   Both of these films show what it was like when Papua New Guineans and white people met for the first time, and the changes that have taken place since then.

7. The Second World War

Many European countries fought between 1914 and 1918. The fighting did not just take place in Europe. This fighting became known as the First World War. Germany lost land and became less powerful after this war. In Chapter 5 we saw how Germany had to give up control of New Guinea and how Australia was asked by the League of Nations to help New Guinea.

The Start of the Second World War

The Second World War began in Europe in 1939. It took two and a half years to reach Papua New Guinea.

When the war started in Europe, Australia sent many men to help Britain fight the Germans. Before this, however, Japan had attacked its neighbours in China, Korea, and Manchuria. America tried to punish Japan by refusing to sell it oil, and by taking away the property owned by Japanese people living in America. This made the Japanese very angry. Japan decided to capture the oil fields in Indonesia and fought against a number of countries, including America, to get this oil.

The fighting reached Papua New Guinea on 23 January 1942 when Japanese soldiers landed at Rabaul. Port Moresby was bombed by the Japanese for the first time on 3 February 1942.

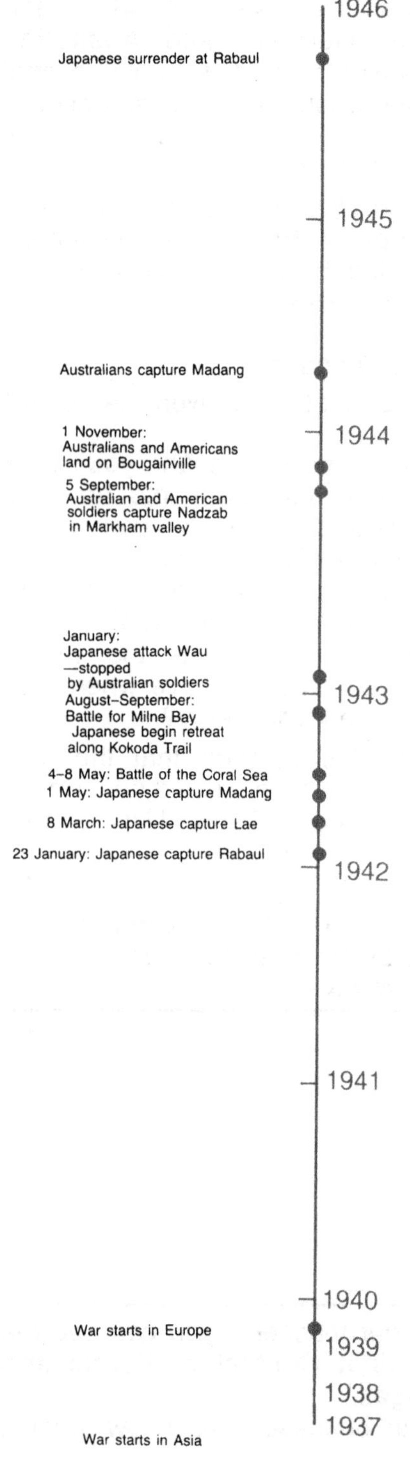

The war in Papua New Guinea.

The Second World War and the Pacific

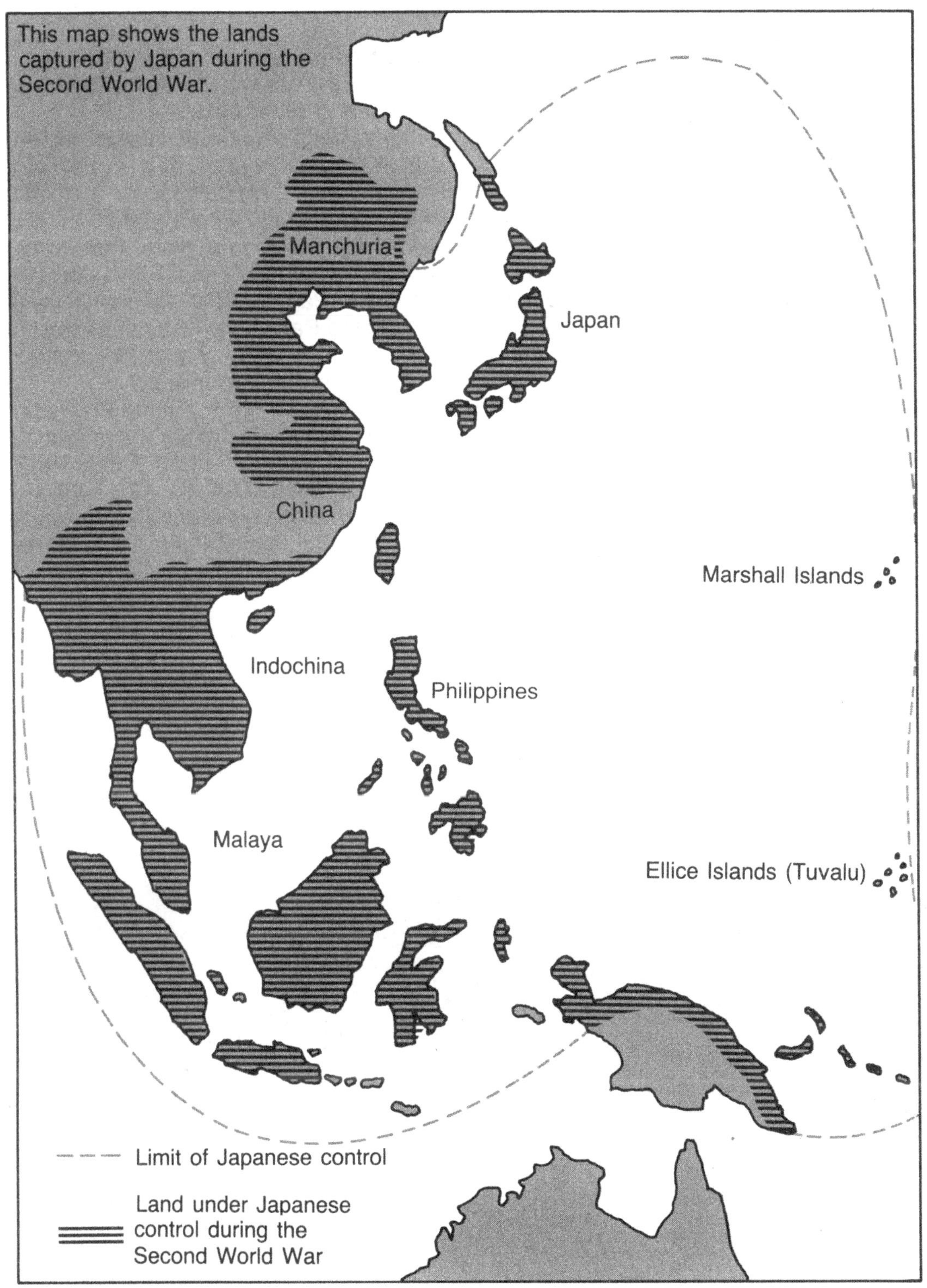

Papua New Guineans and the War

After the First World War, Papua New Guineans saw Australians take the place of Germans. Just 25 years later they saw Japanese take the place of Australians. Papua New Guineans could not tell how long the Japanese would stay. They did not know what was happening in the rest of the world, or even in the rest of Papua New Guinea. Many Papua New Guineans became very confused.

The Second World War brought many changes to Papua New Guinea. Many Papua New Guineans helped the Australian and American soldiers by becoming soldiers, carriers, and guides. They visited places far away from their own village, saw many new things and heard many new ideas. After the war some Papua New Guineans tried to get for their own villages the things that they had seen in other places.

Many **Black American** soldiers helped Australia and America during the war. Papua New Guineans saw that the Black Americans were treated in the same way as other soldiers. Before the war, some Germans and Australians did not treat Papua New Guineans very well. Some Papua New Guineans began to think that they should be treated better when the war finished.

The Papua New Guineans who worked as soldiers, carriers, and guides were paid money. Other Papua New Guineans sold food to the soldiers. There was more money in most villages after the war than before. This money

Many Papua New Guineans became soldiers, carriers, and guides.

was sometimes used to start the first businesses owned by Papua New Guineans.

The Second World War caused many Australians to change the way they thought about Papua New Guinea. Newspapers, books and films about the war told Australians what Papua New Guinea was like. Many Australians were thankful for the help that Papua New Guineans gave Australian soldiers. After the war the Australian people were willing to have more of their money spent helping the people of Papua New Guinea.

What Happened after the War?

After the Second World War finished in 1945, many colonies of European countries asked for **independence**.

Not many people in 1945 thought that Papua New Guinea would be independent just 30 years later. But, as a result of the war, the Australian government started many projects to bring political and economic **development** to Papua New Guinea. It was possible to prepare Papua New Guinea for Independence so quickly only because of the changes caused by the Second World War.

In the next chapter we shall look at some of the big changes that took place between 1945 and Independence in 1975.

Activities

Exercises

1. Name three countries that took part in the fighting in Papua New Guinea during the Second World War.
2. List some of the changes that happened in Papua New Guinea as a result of the Second World War.

Things to Discuss

1. As a class, discuss how you think the history of Papua New Guinea might have been different if the Second World War had not taken place.
2. Why do you think that the last part of this chapter says: "It was possible to prepare Papua New Guinea for Independence so quickly only because of the changes caused by the Second World War."

Things to Do

1. List three good things and three bad things that happened in Papua New Guinea as a result of the Second World War. Write your answer in a table like this:

Results of the Second World War	
Good	**Bad**

2. See if you can find any old stories from your area about the Second World War. Ask the old people in your village if any fighting took place in your area, or if they know of any stories about people from your village who went away to help the soldiers.
3. Ask your teacher if you can see the film **Angels of War**. This film shows some of the effects that the Second World War had on the lives of Papua New Guineans.

8. The Road to Independence

The First Elections

The word **independent** means **free** and **able to do things for yourself**. One of the first things that Australia did after the Second World War to prepare Papua New Guinea for political independence was to give Papua New Guineans the chance to **elect** people to take part in the work of government. Some Papua New Guineans became members of a Local Government Council. The first Local Government Councils were started in 1950 in Hanuabada Village near Port Moresby, in Baluan in Manus Province, and on the Gazelle Peninsula in East New Britain. By 1969 Local Government Councils represented 85 per cent of Papua New Guineans.

Local Government Councils were started to get people from different villages to work together for the development of their area. The Councils also helped to teach people about the way in which the new type of government worked.

A meeting of the Asaro District Local Government Council (outside Goroka).

Uniting the Nation

Before the Second World War, Papua and New Guinea were **administered** by Australia as separate **territories**. They were joined together for the first time in 1949. To help administer the united Papua New Guinea, the **First Legislative Council** was opened on 26 November 1951. This council was like a **parliament**, although the Administrator still had a lot of power. Most members were chosen by the Administrator. Three Papua New Guineans were chosen to be members of the First Legislative Council. It was not until 1961 that Papua New Guineans had the chance to vote for representatives in the Legislative Council.

A meeting of the First Legislative Council.

Sir John Guise when he was Speaker.

National Elections

In 1964 the Legislative Council was increased in size and it changed its name to the **House of Assembly**. Forty-four of the 64 members of the House of Assembly were elected. The other 20 members were chosen by the Administrator. There were 38 Papua New Guineans in the First House of Assembly, but no political parties.

Sir John Guise was the first Papua New Guinean Speaker of the House of Assembly.

In 1968 the House of Assembly was increased in size to 94 members. Of the six political parties that were started in 1967, only one, the Pangu Pati, is still here. After elections in 1972 members of the Pangu Pati joined with other parties to become a **coalition** led by the Chief Minister Michael Somare. Australia still had control over Papua New Guinea.

Two months after these elections, Mr Somare said that a group of people would write a **Constitution** so that Papua New Guinea could become independent soon.

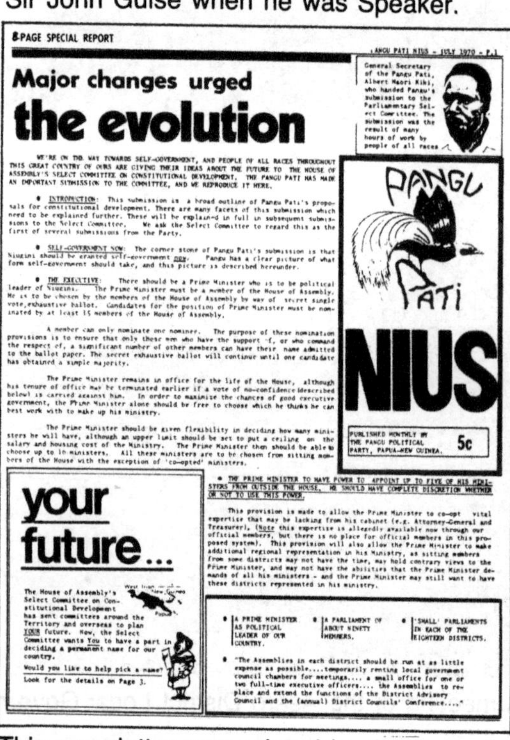

8-PAGE SPECIAL REPORT

PANGU PATI NIUS - JULY 1970 - P.1

Major changes urged

the evolution

General Secretary of the Pangu Pati, Albert Maori Kiki, who handed Pangu's submission to the Parliamentary Select Committee. The submission was the result of many hours of work by people of all races

WE'RE ON THE WAY TOWARDS SELF-GOVERNMENT, AND PEOPLE OF ALL RACES THROUGHOUT THIS GREAT COUNTRY OF OURS ARE GIVING THEIR IDEAS ABOUT THE FUTURE TO THE HOUSE OF ASSEMBLY'S SELECT COMMITTEE ON CONSTITUTIONAL DEVELOPMENT. THE PANGU PATI HAS MADE AN IMPORTANT SUBMISSION TO THE COMMITTEE, AND WE REPRODUCE IT HERE.

● INTRODUCTION: This submission is a broad outline of Pangu Pati's proposals for constitutional development. There are many facets of this submission which need to be explained further. These will be explained in full in subsequent submissions to the Select Committee. We ask the Select Committee to regard this as the first of several submissions from the Party.

● SELF-GOVERNMENT NOW: The corner stone of Pangu Pati's submission is that Niugini should be granted self-government now. Pangu has a clear picture of what form self-government should take, and this picture is described hereunder.

● THE EXECUTIVE: There should be a Prime Minister who is to be political leader of Niugini. The Prime Minister must be a member of the House of Assembly. He is to be chosen by the members of the House of Assembly by way of secret single vote, exhaustive ballot. Candidates for the position of Prime Minister must be nominated by at least 15 members of the House of Assembly.

A member can only nominate one nominee. The purpose of these nomination provisions is to ensure that only these men who have the support of, or who command the respect of, a significant number of other members can have their name admitted to the ballot paper. The secret exhaustive ballot will continue until one candidate has obtained a simple majority.

The Prime Minister remains in office for the life of the House, although his tenure of office may be terminated earlier if a vote of no-confidence (described below) is carried against him. In order to maximize the chances of good executive government, the Prime Minister alone should be free to choose which he thinks he can best work with to make up his ministry.

The Prime Minister should be given flexibility in deciding how many ministers he will have, although an upper limit should be set to put a ceiling on the salary and housing cost of the Ministry. The Prime Minister then should be able to choose up to 10 ministers. All these ministers are to be chosen from sitting members of the House with the exception of 'co-opted' ministers.

PANGU PATI

NIUS

PUBLISHED MONTHLY BY THE PANGU POLITICAL PARTY, PAPUA-NEW GUINEA. 5c

● THE PRIME MINISTER TO HAVE POWER TO APPOINT UP TO FIVE OF HIS MINISTERS FROM OUTSIDE THE HOUSE. HE SHOULD HAVE COMPLETE DISCRETION WHETHER OR NOT TO USE THIS POWER.

This provision is made to allow the Prime Minister to co-opt vital expertise that may be lacking from his cabinet (e.g. Attorney-General and Treasurer). (Note this expertise is allegedly available now through our official members, but there is no place for official members in this proposed system). This provision will also allow the Prime Minister to make additional regional representation in his Ministry, as sitting members from some districts may not have the time, may hold contrary views to the Prime Minister, and may not have the abilities that the Prime Minister demands of all his ministers - and the Prime Minister may still want to have these districts represented in his ministry.

your future...

The House of Assembly's Select Committee on Constitutional Development has sent committees around the Territory and overseas to plan YOUR future. Now, the Select Committee wants You to have a part in deciding a permanent name for our country.

Would you like to help pick a name?

Look for the details on Page 3.

● A PRIME MINISTER AS POLITICAL LEADER OF OUR COUNTRY.

● A PARLIAMENT OF ABOUT NINETY MEMBERS.

● 'SMALL' PARLIAMENTS IN EACH OF THE EIGHTEEN DISTRICTS.

● "The Assemblies in each district should be run at as little expense as possible....temporarily renting local government council chambers for meetings.... a small office for one or two full-time executive officers.... the Assemblies to replace and extend the functions of the District Advisory Council and the (annual) District Councils' Conference...."

This newsletter was printed by the Pangu Pati and explains their policy of wanting self-government.

Independence

Papua New Guinea became **self-governing** on 1 December 1973. Defence, the work of the Supreme Court, and Papua New Guinea's relations with other countries were still controlled by Australia. It was not until the Constitution was finished towards the end of 1975 that Independence finally came. The Australian flag was taken down for the last time on the night of 15 September 1975. Papua New Guinea became an independent country on 16 September 1975, with Michael Somare as the first Prime Minister.

Mr Somare signing the papers which gave Papua New Guinea self-government. He is watched by the last Australian Administrator, Mr Les Johnson.

This photograph shows Sir John Guise taking down the Australian flag for the last time on the afternoon of 15 September 1975.

Papua New Guinea: political development.

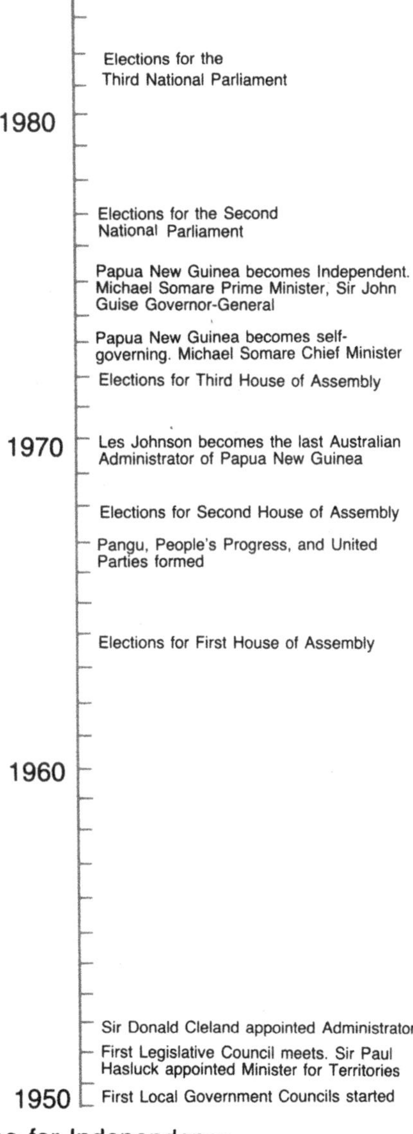

Time-line for Independence.

PAPUA NEW GUINEA
Post-Courier

Incorporating South Pacific Post and New Guinea Times Courier.
PO Box 85 Port Moresby

36 Pages — TUESDAY, SEPTEMBER 16, 1975 — 10 toea

Phone: Port Moresby 25 9890 — Lae 42 4168 — Rabaul 92 1244

IT'S OUR DAY

Papua New Guinea became independent today with this proclamation of Independence by the Governor General, Sir John Guise:

"Distinguished guests, visitors from overseas, people of Papua New Guinea:

"Papua New Guinea is now independent.

"The Constitution of the Independent State of Papua New Guinea under which all power rests with the people is now in effect.

"We have at this point of time broken with our colonial past and we now stand as an independent nation in our own right.

"Let us unite with the Almighty God's guidance and help in working together for the future as a strong and free country."

● THE Australian flag went down for the last time in Papua New Guinea yesterday. Today, the Papua New Guinea flag will be raised for the world's newest country.

No. 1097 Registered at the GPO Port Moresby for transmission by post as a qualified publication.

Activities

Exercises

1. Copy and complete the crossword puzzle below.

Across

6. Free and able to do things for yourself.
9. First Papua New Guinean to be Speaker in the House of Assembly.
10. One of the first provinces to have local Government Councils.
11. A group of people who share similar political ideas.
13. Chief Minister during self-government and first Prime Minister of Papua New Guinea.
14. Local Government Councils tried to get the people to ______ together to develop their area.

Down

1. A word which means to govern or look after.
2. Local Government Councils were started to give ______ people the chance to take part in the work of government.
3. A way of choosing representatives in government.
4. A country which administered Papua New Guinea before Independence.
5. A set of ideas used to help with the running of a country.
7. One of the first political parties to be started in Papua New Guinea.
8. On 1 December 1973 Papua New Guinea became ______ governing.
11. At Independence the ______ to govern Papua New Guinea was taken from Australia and given to Papua New Guinea.
12. Another word for independent.

Things to Discuss

1. Read the following two quotations:

> "It is hoped that Papua New Guineans will begin by taking more control over matters affecting their own villages. Later they may get some sort of self-government for the country as a whole. . . . That is a long way ahead. It may take, as I have said, more than 100 years."
>
> Hon. Paul Hasluck
> Australian Minister for Territories, 1951.

> "Self-government is coming. We want it as soon as possible. The time has come when our people are ready to govern our country. Once they do this and are seen to do it well, these people who are now worried will be happy and support their leaders."
>
> Michael Somare
> Chief Minister, 1972.

(a) Why did some people think that Independence would take a long time to come to Papua New Guinea?

(b) Do you think that Papua New Guinea was well prepared for Independence?

2. What does the word "independence" mean to you?

Things to Do

1. Some Papua New Guineans thought that Independence was given to Papua New Guinea too soon.

Imagine that the year is 1975. List three arguments for and three arguments against giving Independence to Papua New Guinea at that time. Write your answer in a table like this:

Independence	
Arguments For Independence in 1975	**Arguments Against Independence in 1975**

This cartoon shows some of the groups who did not want Independence for Papua New Guinea in 1975, or who wanted to break away from the rest of Papua New Guinea.

9. Independent Papua New Guinea

Provincial Government

Today, many of the decisions made in Papua New Guinea are made by Provincial Governments and Local Government Councils. Sharing power between the National, Provincial, and Local governments is known as **decentralisation**. This means that some of the power is taken away from the National Government. The reason for this is to give as many people as possible the chance to take part in the work of government.

Decentralisation was first talked about in Papua New Guinea during the 1960s. Bougainville said in the early 1970s that it would break away or **secede** from the rest of Papua New Guinea unless it was given more power to run itself. A law was passed in July 1974 to allow a type of Provincial Government to be started in Bougainville. The new province was called North Solomons Province. Today all 19 provinces have a Provincial Government.

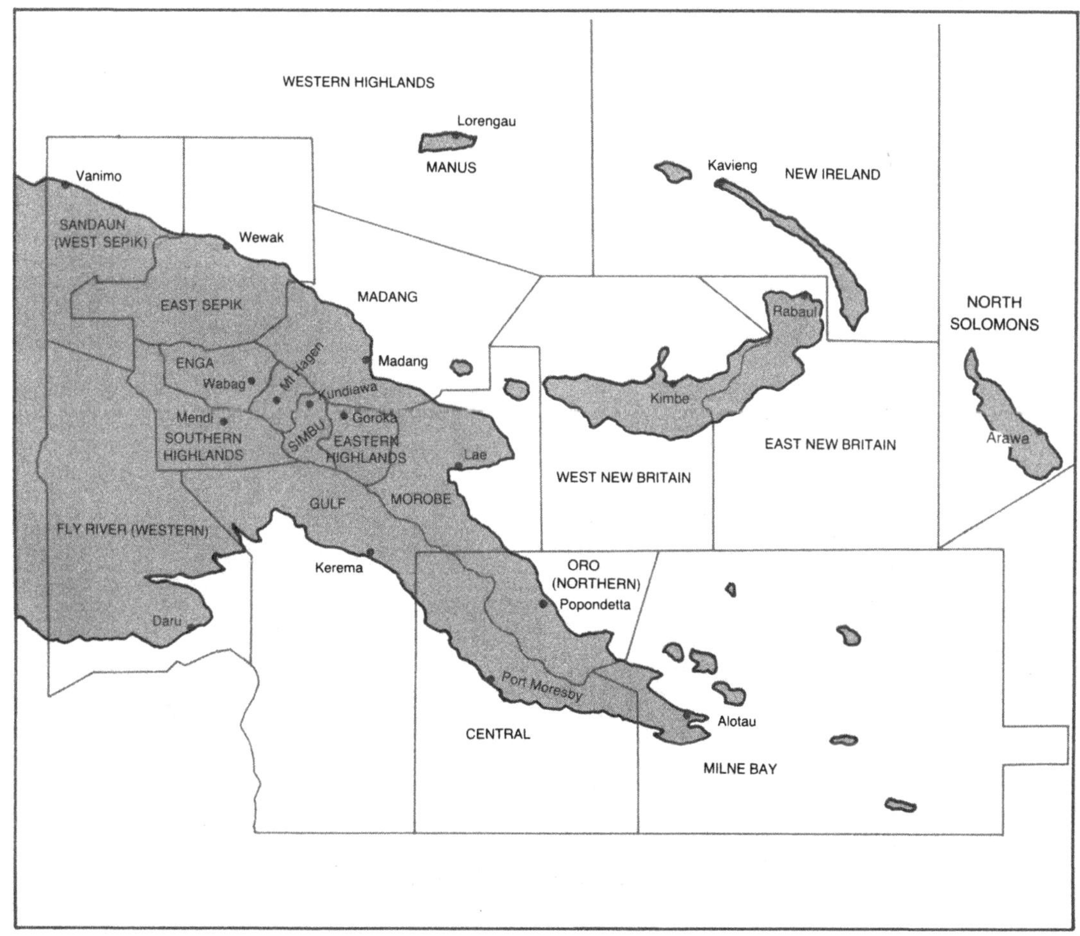

Provinces and Provincial capitals.

Economic Development

The people of Papua New Guinea have done many things to make our country a better place to live. Roads and airstrips have been built, and radio and telephone **services** have been provided. These help to improve communications between different parts of Papua New Guinea. More and more children have the chance to go to school. Most people can now get help for health problems at an aidpost or health centre.

Building roads.

More and more children have the chance to go to school.

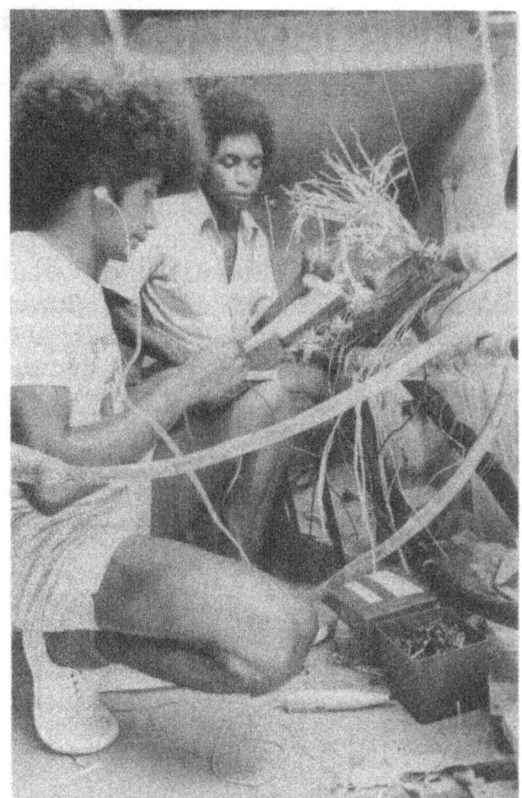

Providing telephone services.

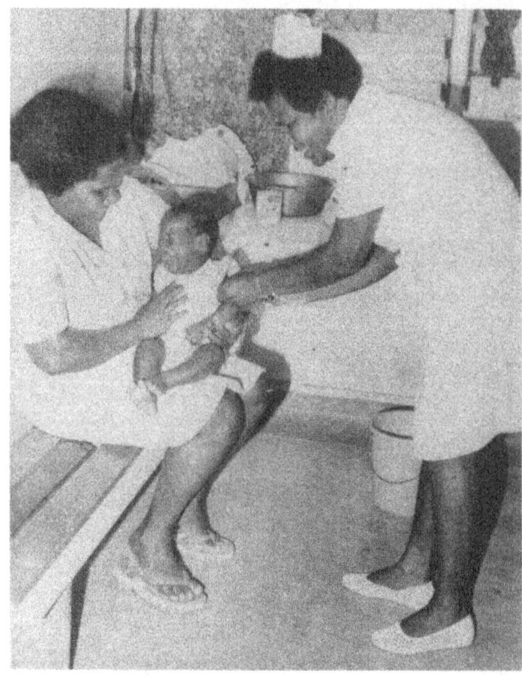

Help for health problems.

Many types of business have been started. A lot of these businesses are owned by Papua New Guineans. Some of these businesses are owned by people from other countries.

These businesses give work to Papua New Guineans who are able to use the money that they get to make their lives better. Sometimes these businesses produce things such as coffee, copper, or fish, which can be sold to other countries. These **exports** earn money which Papua New Guinea can use to buy the **imports** that we need from other countries.

Destination of our exports, 1984.

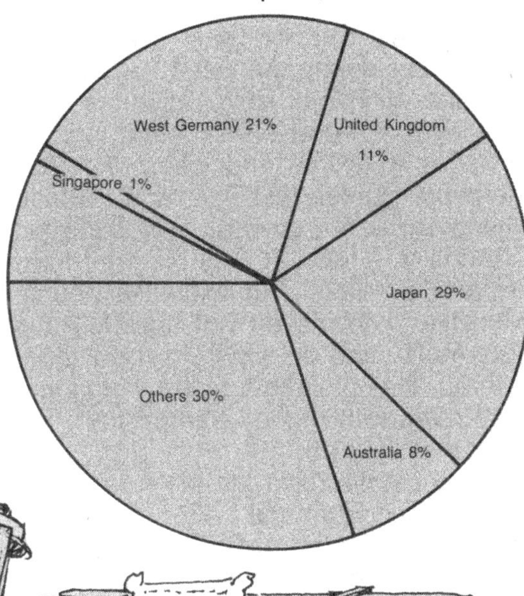

Some of our main exports.

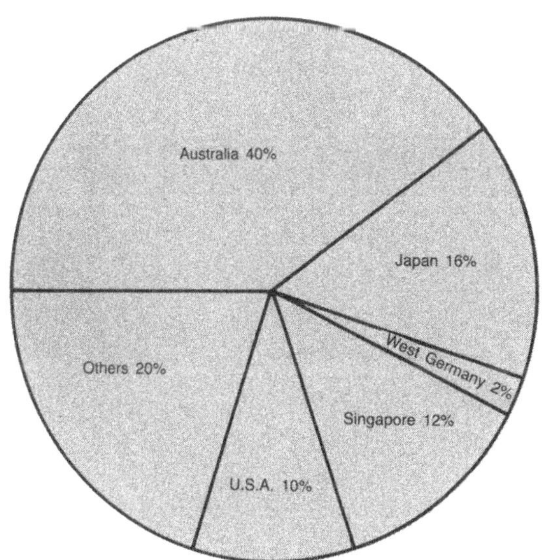

Sources of our imports, 1984.

Some things we import.

Towns and Cities

Papua New Guinea has changed in many ways during the last 100 years. In the past, all Papua New Guineans lived in villages in **rural** areas. Many people now live in towns and cities like Port Moresby, Goroka, Wewak, and Rabaul. These towns are growing very quickly.

Living in a town is very different from living in a village. For example, people who live in towns do not usually have very much land on which to grow food. Instead, they buy most of the things that they need with money earned from the work that they do.

Many people have left the rural areas to try to find work and better services in the towns. Not all of these people are able to find work or a place to live. Some of these people have built houses on land which they do not own. Where there are many of these houses the area is called a **squatter settlement**.

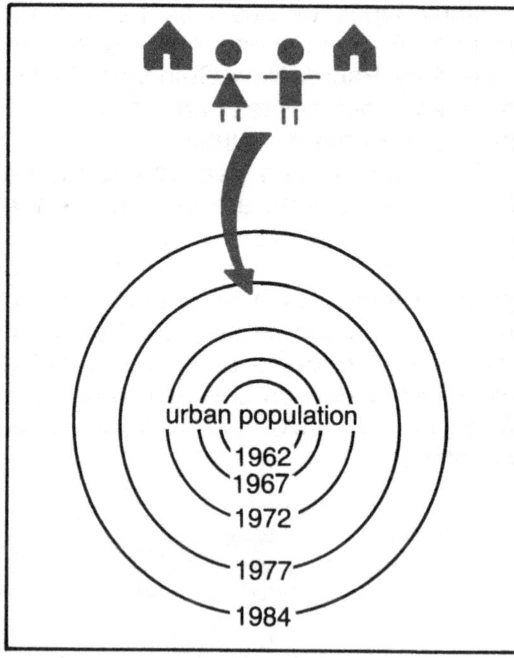

Rural–urban migration, 1962–1984.

A squatter settlement.

In this book we have seen how Papua New Guinea became a united, independent nation. In the last chapter we shall look at how Papua New Guinea works together with other countries.

Activities

Exercises

1. The words to complete these paragraphs are hidden in the puzzle below. See how many of these words you are able to find.

   Provincial Government
   After Independence a system of ______ Government was started in Papua New Guinea. One reason for doing this was to ________ political power, to give more people a chance to take part in the work of government. The first province to get this type of government was ________.

   Economic Development
   Since Independence the Government has provided many ________ to make people's lives better. Many new businesses have been started and Papua New Guinea has begun to ________ a lot with other countries. All of these things have brought economic ______ to Papua New Guinea.

   Towns and Cities
   Most people in Papua New Guinea live in ________ areas. Towns and cities have grown very quickly in Papua New Guinea. Although this has brought some benefits, it has also caused some ________.

T A P R O B L E M S I S
R O R A L I S E M A L E
A D O P A P U N A G A R
D E V E L O P M E N T V
E L I P R I R U A L S I
B A N D E R U R O I E C
D E C E N T R A L I S E
A D I P R A A N W S P S
Y I A E N B L O N S P E
N O L I M A N T O W A N

Things to Discuss

1. As a class, discuss each of the following points of view.

   (a) *Provincial Government*
   "Having Provincial and Local Governments as well as the National Government gives more people a chance to take part in the work of government. This helps to bring development to those areas where it is most needed."

   "There are too many politicians in Papua New Guinea. Many people are confused about what they are supposed to do. As a result a lot of services do not get to the places where they are really needed."

   (b) *Economic Development*
   "Papua New Guinea must try to develop more agriculture and industry as quickly as possible. We must not allow customs and traditions to slow this down."

   "We must make sure that Papua New Guinea develops in a way that helps all Papua New Guineans and protects those customs and traditions which are important."

   (c) *Towns and Cities*
   "The growth of towns and cities in Papua New Guinea is a sign of development. People should be encouraged to come to the towns and cities to have a better life."

   "The rural areas produce most of the things which we use in Papua New Guinea. People should be encouraged to stay in the rural areas to help develop our country."

Things to Do

1. Collect newspaper articles that talk about some of the important changes that are taking place in Papua New Guinea. Group these under the headings **Government**, **People**, and **Economic Development**. Talk about these articles and then display them on your classroom noticeboard.
2. What would you like Papua New Guinea to be like in the future? List the five most important developments that you would like to see in Papua New Guinea over the next ten years.
   Compare your list with the lists that other students have written.

10. Papua New Guinea, Other Countries, and the Future

Papua New Guinea and Australia

Papua New Guinea and Australia have continued to work together since Independence. Papua New Guinea and Australia sell a lot of exports to each other. Each year Australia gives Papua New Guinea a **grant** or gift of money which can be used to provide better services to Papua New Guineans. This grant is an important part of the National Government's budget each year. The size of the grant is being reduced as Papua New Guinea becomes more **self-reliant**.

This post marks the border between Papua New Guinea and Indonesia.

Indonesia

Indonesia is another of Papua New Guinea's neighbours. The western half of the island of New Guinea is a part of Indonesia. It is called Irian Jaya.

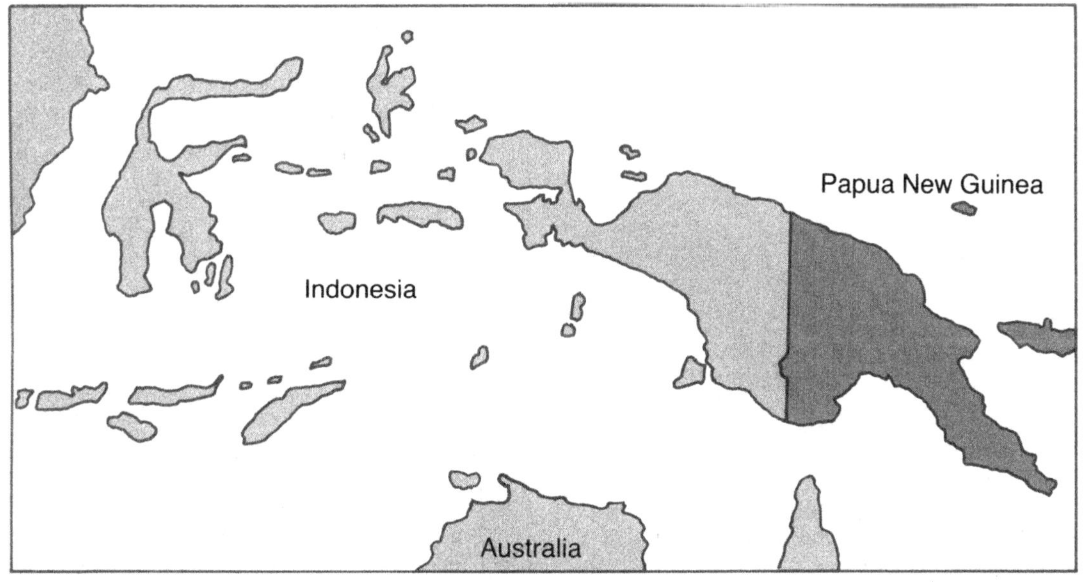

Irian Jayans and Papua New Guineans are Melanesians. People living near the border between Irian Jaya and Papua New Guinea have been visiting and trading with each other for thousands of years. Many have relations living on the other side of the border.

Irian Jaya has been a province of Indonesia since 1963. Most Indonesians are Asians. Some Irian Jayans say that they are not like the other Indonesians. These Irian Jayans want an independent country. They have sometimes fought against Indonesia about this. When there is fighting, people sometimes come to Papua New Guinea for safety. However, Papua New Guinea and Indonesia work together to help each other in many ways.

These people are members of an organisation called the O.P.M. which wants Independence for Irian Jaya.

The then Minister for Foreign Affairs, Mr Rabbie Namaliu, meeting with the Indonesian Minister for Foreign Affairs, Dr Mochtar.

Is Papua New Guinea an Asian or a Pacific Nation?

Papua New Guinea is very close to a number of Asian countries. A lot of the exports and imports that Papua New Guinea buys and sells are from Asia. Asian countries such as Japan have also given Papua New Guinea a lot of help. For example, the Fisheries College at Kavieng was built for Papua New Guinea by Japan.

Some of Papua New Guinea's neighbours have joined an organisation called the Association of South East Asian Nations—ASEAN. ASEAN helps develop trade between member countries. Member countries also work together when they want to start new projects. Although Papua New Guinea is not a member of ASEAN it is invited to ASEAN meetings and works with ASEAN members.

Papua New Guinea is also a Pacific nation. Pacific nations have started a number of organisations to help each other. Papua New Guinea is a member of many of these.

One of these organisations is the South Pacific Forum. Member countries share the knowledge that they have to develop new projects. The Pacific Forum Shipping Line is an example of how Pacific countries, including Papua New Guinea, have worked together to improve transport within the Pacific.

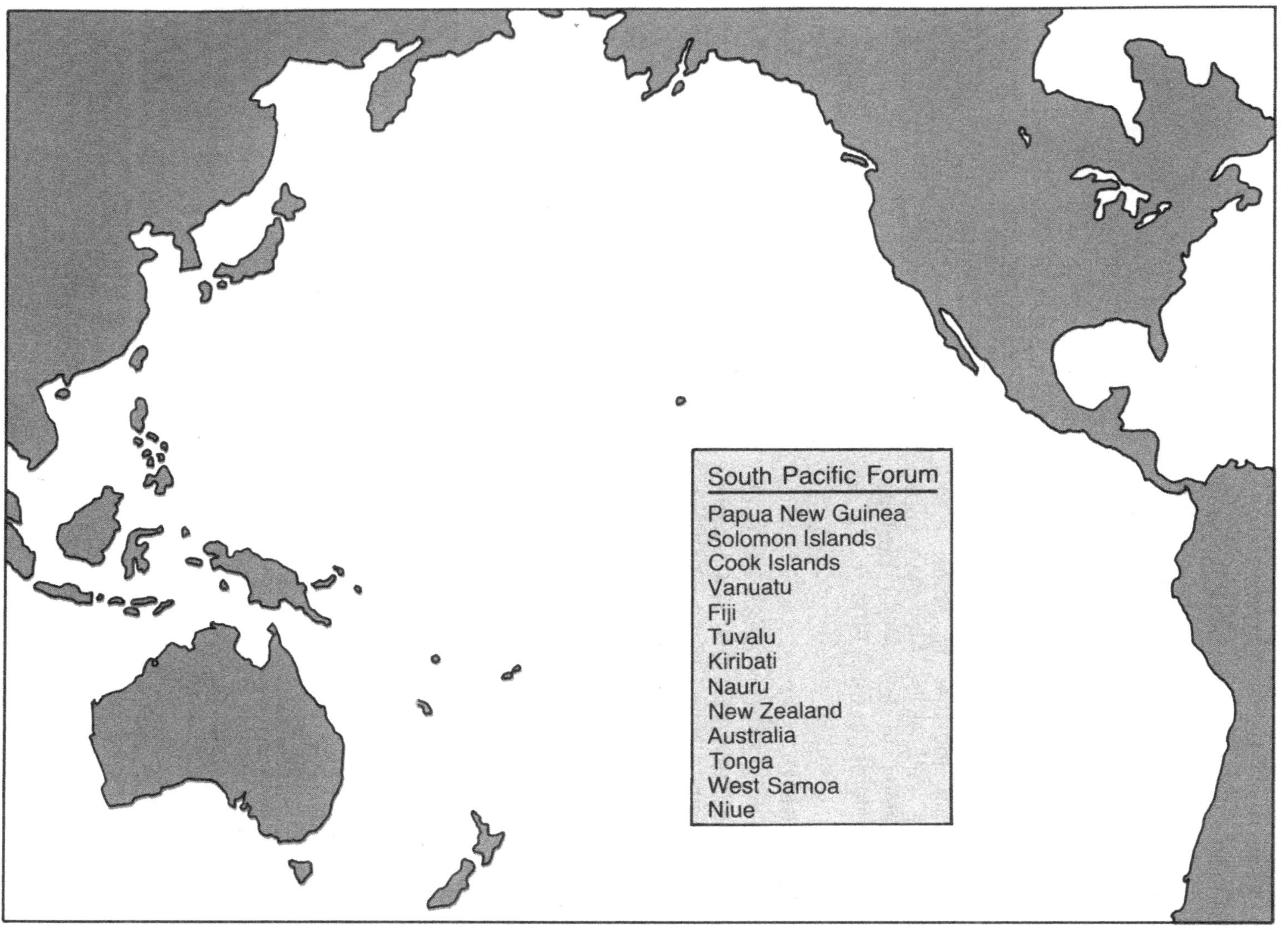
South Pacific Forum
Papua New Guinea
Solomon Islands
Cook Islands
Vanuatu
Fiji
Tuvalu
Kiribati
Nauru
New Zealand
Australia
Tonga
West Samoa
Niue

The British Commonwealth

We saw in Chapter 5 that Australia was once governed by Britain. Many of the countries that were once colonies of Britain have joined an organisation called the British Commonwealth. Papua New Guinea is a member of the British Commonwealth because of its past relationship with both Britain and Australia.

Members of the British Commonwealth work together to share their knowledge and skills. Members also hold meetings to talk about political topics of interest to each other.

This photograph shows leaders of Commonwealth countries at a meeting in Port Moresby in August 1984.

Conclusion

This book has shown us how the land was formed and how the first people came to Papua New Guinea. We have talked about the arrival of the first white people and the new government which they brought. Finally we have seen how Papua New Guinea became the **united** independent nation that it is today.

In your Social Science lessons during the rest of your time at Provincial High School you will look at some of these topics in a little more detail. We hope that you enjoy learning more about our country in your Social Science lessons, and that they will help you to become better **citizens**.

Activities

Exercises

1. List three ways in which Papua New Guinea works together with other countries.
2. Papua New Guinea is a member of the following organisations:
   - the South Pacific Forum
   - the British Commonwealth.

   Papua New Guinea also has the right to observe ASEAN meetings.
   (a) Briefly explain what each of these organisations does.
   (b) Name three other organisations of which Papua New Guinea is a member.

Things to Discuss

1. We have seen how Papua New Guinea became a politically independent country. Do you think that a country could exist without any relations with any other country? If they could, do you think that this would be a good idea?
2. Imagine that you have been asked by the Minister for Foreign Affairs to help write a new foreign policy for Papua New Guinea. Discuss some of the important ideas that you think should be included in this policy. For example, in what ways should Papua New Guinea co-operate with other countries? Should Papua New Guinea join international organisations? What should Papua New Guinea do if it is threatened by war?

Things to Do

1. Pin a large world map to your classroom noticeboard. Collect newspaper articles that talk about Papua New Guinea's relations with other countries. These could include co-operation through trade, sport, politics, and aid. Pin these newspaper articles to the noticeboard and then show with arrows where the country that Papua New Guinea is working with is located.

Glossary

Word	Page	Meaning
administer	36	to manage the affairs of another country.
administrator	25	the Chief Executive Officer in both German New Guinea (1885) and British Papua (1888).
ancestor	15	relatives who lived a long time ago.
archaeologist	11	a scientist who studies places where people lived long ago.
artifacts	2	things such as tools and weapons made by people.
Black Americans	33	people who now live in America but who have ancestors who came from Africa.
catechists	28	people who helped the missionaries to teach and spread the Christian religion.
citizens	50	members of a country.
coalition	36	two or more political parties joined together to form a government.
colony	20	country ruled by another country.
constitution	36	the written rules which set out how a country should be governed.
custom	1	the traditional or usual way of doing something.
decentralisation	41	giving some power to lower levels of government.
development	33	changing for improvement.
elect	35	to choose a person by voting.
eruption	4	when melted rock comes up through the earth's surface.
evangelists	28	people who helped the missionaries to teach and spread the Christian religion.
evidence	5	facts that explain or prove something.
explorer	16	a person who travels to an unknown place to find out more about it.
exports	43	products that a country sells to another country.
foreign policy	31	the rules a government makes for carrying out its business with other countries.
geologist	4	a scientist who studies rocks.
government	17	the elected group of people who organise the nation's affairs.
grant	47	a gift of money Australia gives to Papua New Guinea to provide better services to Papua New Guinea.
history	1	the study of past events—political, social, economic.
House of Assembly	36	the old name for our National Parliament; the place where elected members of parliament met to discuss how the country should be run.
imports	43	products that a country buys from other countries.
independence	37	the power to govern our own country without being controlled by other countries.

Word	Page	Meaning
independent	20	free from the control of another country.
labour recruiter	17	person who finds others to do work.
League of Nations	21	an organisation that was formed after World War I to try to keep world peace. This is now called the United Nations.
legend	3	a traditional story.
Legislative Council	36	government body whose main function was to advise the Administrator on matters affecting the Territory.
luluai	27	a village person who was appointed to make sure that people followed the European laws.
missionaries	17	people who spread religion.
opinion	29	a point of view or idea.
oral history	2	stories, songs, and poetry which provide useful information about our past.
parliament	36	the chief law-making body of a country.
patrol officer	26	an officer who tried to bring peace into an area before colonial government could start its work.
peninsula	12	a piece of land nearly surrounded by water.
protectorate	20	a country placed under the care of another country.
rural	44	something to do with the countryside; areas away from the towns.
Sahul	8	the piece of land which was made up of modern Australia and Papua New Guinea joined together.
secede	41	to break away from a country in order to form a new country.
self-governing	37	ruling oneself, without outside help.
self-reliant	47	able to make by itself most of the things that a country needs and wants.
services	42	things that people need in everyday life that are provided by the government.
spices	16	plants that are used to flavour food, such as nutmeg, cloves, cinnamon, cardamom, and ginger.
squatters	44	people who illegally live on unoccupied land that they do not own.
territories	36	land or countries ruled by one government.
trade	17	the buying and selling of goods.
traders	15	people who buy and sell goods.
tradition	1	handing down of beliefs and customs from one generation to another.
tultul	27	assistants to luluais. Tultuls were village officials who acted mainly as interpreters.
united	36	joined together or acting together.

Index